T3-BHD-778

The Writing Prompts Workbook, Grades 1-2:
Story Starters for Journals, Assignments and More

Bryan Cohen

This publication is protected under the US Copyright Act of 1976 and all other applicable international, federal, state and local laws, and all rights are reserved, including resale rights: you are not allowed to give or sell this book to anyone else. If you received this publication from anyone other than Bryan Cohen, Amazon or Build Creative Writing Ideas, you've received a pirated copy. Please contact us via the website and notify us of the situation.

All contents Copyright © 2012 by Build Creative Writing Ideas and Bryan Cohen. All rights reserved. No part of this document or the related files may be reproduced or transmitted in any form, by any means (electronic, photocopying, recording, or otherwise) without the prior written permission of the publisher.

Limit of Liability and Disclaimer of Warranty: The publisher has used its best efforts in preparing this book, and the information provided herein is provided "as is." Bryan Cohen and Build Creative Writing Ideas make no representation or warranties with respect to the accuracy or completeness of the contents of this book and specifically disclaims any implied warranties of merchantability or fitness for any particular purpose and shall in no event be liable for any loss of profit or any other commercial damage, including but not limited to special, incidental, consequential, or other damages. All characters appearing in this work are fictitious. Any resemblance to real persons, living or dead, is purely coincidental.

Trademarks: This book identifies product names and services known to be trademarks, registered trademarks, or service marks of their respective holders. They are used throughout this book in an editorial fashion only. In addition, terms suspected of being trademarks, registered trademarks, or service marks have been appropriately capitalized, although Bryan Cohen and Build Creative Writing Ideas cannot attest to the accuracy of this information. Use of a term in this book should not be regarded as affecting the validity of any trademark, registered trademark, or service mark. Bryan Cohen and Build Creative Writing Ideas are not associated with any product or vendor mentioned in this book.

Finally, use your head. Nothing in this book is intended to replace common sense, legal, medical or other professional advice, and is meant to inform and entertain the reader. So have fun with the book and happy writing!

Edited by Debra Cohen and Amy Crater.

Copyright © 2012 Build Creative Writing Ideas and Bryan Cohen

All rights reserved.

ISBN: 0985482206
ISBN-13: 978-0-9854822-0-6

DEDICATION

I dedicate this book to my parents and teachers who left me alone with my workbooks and let my imagination run wild.

CONTENTS

INTRODUCTION

Welcome to *The Writing Prompts Workbook*! Within these pages you'll find 200 writing prompts, two on each page, that will help to stimulate the imagination of your students or children. I've found that the key to allowing students to fully latch onto an idea is to give them a scenario followed by a question. In answering the question, young writers can take the same prompt a million different directions. You may even want to try photocopying a page and have your writers take on the same prompt at the beginning and the end of a school year just to see how different their storytelling has become.

The Writing Prompts Workbook series is a collection of books I've created after seeing how many parents and teachers have visited my website, Build Creative Writing Ideas (located at http://www.build-creative-writing-ideas.com). I have adapted my thousands of prompts into six workbooks designed to take a first grader creatively all the way up through the end of high school. The six books are available for grades 1-2, 3-4, 5-6, 7-8, 9-10 and 11-12. The prompts become more complex with each volume, but continue to remain imaginative and creative throughout.

I love hearing about the progress of students on my site and I'm always interested in hearing new ideas for delivering creative writing prompts to writers from the ages of five to 105. Feel free to contact me on my website for any questions and comments you can think of. I hope you and your future best-selling authors thoroughly enjoy this and future books in the series. Happy writing!

Sincerely,
Bryan Cohen
Author of *The Writing Prompts Workbook* Series

PS: While there is space below each prompt for your budding writers to write, there is a good chance they may have more to say than they can fit on the page. There is an extra lined page in the back if you'd like to photocopy it, but I strongly suggest that you also get a notebook and some extra pencils just in case. A dictionary for words they don't know yet may also be helpful.

Name _____ Date _____

1. There are so many different places you can go in a single day.
You might just go to school and home. But on some days you could go to the post office, the mall, to music class or even to your grandmother's house! What are the five places you go to the most and what do you like about them?

_____

_____

_____

_____

_____

2. One of the best times of the day is when you get to sit down and have a meal like breakfast, lunch or dinner. What is the tastiest meal you've ever had? How often would you have it if you had a choice? What would happen if you tried cooking it yourself?

_____

_____

_____

_____

©2012 Build Creative Writing Ideas

Name _____ Date _____

3. Who are some of the most important people in your life? What are
the ways in which you show them that you care about them? What are three new things
you could do to make them happy in the next week or two?

_____

_____

_____

_____

4. Of all the people you know, who has the nicest eyes? Who has the biggest smile? Who is
the strongest? Who is the fastest? Who is the smartest? What would it be like if one person
had all of those qualities? What would that person be like?

_____

_____

_____

_____

©2012 Build Creative Writing Ideas

Name _____ Date _____

5. Sometimes kids your age have a tough life because their family
doesn't have a lot of money, they live in a rough area or they have some medical problems.
If you could do something about their situation, what would you do and why?

_____

_____

_____

_____

6. What is your favorite thing in the whole wide world to do and why? Do any of your
friends like to do the same activity? Describe a day in which you and you friends could do
the activity all day long.

_____

_____

_____

_____

©2012 Build Creative Writing Ideas

Name _____ Date _____

7. Who do you think is the coolest celebrity and/or movie star in the world? What do you think an average day would be like for this famous person?

_____

_____

_____

_____

8. There are so many different places in the world that it would be close to impossible to see every country in your lifetime. If you could pick five different countries to go do during your life, what would they be and why?

_____

_____

_____

_____

©2012 Build Creative Writing Ideas

Name _____ Date _____

9. Who are your three best friends? Write at least a sentence about why each of them is a great friend to you.

_____

_____

_____

_____

_____

10. What is the most fun you have ever had with your friends? Was it a party? Was it a trip somewhere? Perhaps, it was just a few of you hanging out? Talk about the event from beginning to end and why it was so fun.

_____

_____

_____

_____

_____

©2012 Build Creative Writing Ideas

Name _____ Date _____

11. Imagine that your best friend has to move away from home for
an entire year. He or she will be back, but you need to keep in touch via letters because
there are no computers there. Write your first letter to your friend to tell him or her some
things going on in your life and town.

_____

_____

_____

_____

12. What are a few of the things that make you a good and loyal friend? What good things
would your best friends say about you?

_____

_____

_____

_____

©2012 Build Creative Writing Ideas

Name _____ Date _____

13. If you could hang out with your friends anywhere within driving distance, where would it be? What would you guys do there and what would you talk about while hanging out?

_____

_____

_____

_____

14. Imagine that you and your friends stay close for the rest of your lives and you have a big reunion when you all turn 40 years old. Perhaps you'll now be married, have kids and jobs. Write a little scene between the 40-year-old versions of you and your friends at this reunion.

_____

_____

_____

_____

 ©2012 Build Creative Writing Ideas

Name _____ Date _____

15. Look around you and in your head; pick someone that you don't
really know but that you think you'd get along with pretty well. Write a story about how
the two of you might become friends.

_____

_____

_____

_____

_____

16. What is friendship and what does it take to be a good friend? If someone didn't have
these good qualities, what would they have to do to get them?

_____

_____

_____

_____

_____

©2012 Build Creative Writing Ideas

Name _____ Date _____

17. You have been befriended by a group of kids that are a couple of years older than you. They ask you to come and hang out with them. What do you and your new friends do together that the friends your age wouldn't normally do? Describe this time from beginning to end.

_____

_____

_____

_____

18. Some people have lots of different groups of friends. They might have their school friends, camp friends, church or synagogue friends, etc. What would it be like if all your different friends from all your different groups got together and had a party? Which friends would get along and which wouldn't?

_____

_____

_____

_____

©2012 Build Creative Writing Ideas

Name _____ Date _____

19. What is the first present you remember getting for your birthday?
Was it exactly what you wanted? How often did you use it?

_____

_____

_____

_____

_____

20. Everyone knows that if you blow out the candles on your cake you get at least one free wish. If you had one birthday wish for your next birthday, what would it be and why? Talk about what would happen if the wish came true.

_____

_____

_____

_____

_____

©2012 Build Creative Writing Ideas

Name _____ Date _____

21. Describe your perfect birthday party. Would there be clowns? Would there be video games? How many friends would be there? Be specific and write about everything that would and could happen during the party.

_____

_____

_____

_____

22. What is the best present that you and your parents have picked out for another person's birthday? How did you go about picking the most appropriate gift possible? Does it feel good giving something special to someone else?

_____

_____

_____

_____

 ©2012 Build Creative Writing Ideas

Name _____ Date _____

23. How is the birthday party for a kid's birthday different from an adult's birthday party? Do you think the adults have as much fun as the kids?

_____

_____

_____

_____

24. Which birthday do you think is the most important one? Is it turning 10 because you have 2 digits? Is it 15 because you get to go to high school? Write a story about your birthday party the day you turn that special age.

_____

_____

_____

_____

   ©2012 Build Creative Writing Ideas

Name _____ Date _____

25. Imagine that you have to plan the birthday party for your best
friend. What are the special things that you would plan? Remember that this is a party for
your best friend, so make sure to include all the things he or she likes.

_____

_____

_____

_____

_____

26. What is the most memorable birthday cake you've ever seen? What made it so special?
What was its flavor and how big was it? How many pieces of it would you have if you had
the choice?

_____

_____

_____

_____

_____

                                               ©2012 *Build Creative Writing Ideas*

Name _____ Date _____

27. After escaping prison, a group of robbers have taken your cake and all your presents. What are you going to do? Write a story about how you and your friends save your birthday party.

_____

_____

_____

_____

28. If you could invite anyone from history, from television, or from movies to your birthday party, who would it be and why? What gifts would they bring you? What would you talk about?

_____

_____

_____

_____

©2012 Build Creative Writing Ideas

Name _____ Date _____

29. Who is your favorite cartoon character and why? Imagine that you and this character went on an amazing adventure together. Talk about the entire day in which you are together from beginning to end.

_____

_____

_____

_____

30. What would your day be like if it was animated like a cartoon? Would you bounce and fly to school? Would your teachers and classmates make funny faces all day long? Describe your world as if it was a cartoon in full detail.

_____

_____

_____

_____

 ©2012 Build Creative Writing Ideas

Name _____ Date _____

31. Some cartoons have wacky sound effects that make everybody laugh. Imagine that everything you did was accompanied by a silly and strange sound. What are some of the sounds and how would you feel about everyone around you laughing all the time?

_____

_____

_____

_____

32. You are an animated super hero ready to take on the world and stop bad guys. What special powers would you possess? What would a day in your new super heroic life be like?

_____

_____

_____

_____

©2012 Build Creative Writing Ideas

Name _____ Date _____

33. Describe what a cartoon version of you would look like. Talk about your hair and your face and your clothes. What would your animated room look like? Tell every detail possible.

_____

_____

_____

_____

_____

34. You have been captured by an evil cartoon villain! Luckily, all of your favorite cartoons from different shows are coming together to rescue you. Who are the villains and who are the heroes in this story? How do they eventually rescue you from the clutches of evil?

_____

_____

_____

_____

_____

 ©2012 Build Creative Writing Ideas

Name _____ Date _____

35. If you worked for an animation company, what type of cartoon would you make? Try to come up with something original that has never been done before!

_____

_____

_____

_____

_____

36. Slowly but surely, everything in the world has started to become animated and you have to stop it. What do you do to discover what is causing everyone to become hand-drawn and how do you keep it from taking over?

_____

_____

_____

_____

_____

©2012 Build Creative Writing Ideas

Name _____ Date _____

37. If you could make one cartoon character come to the real world
who would it be and why? Since this is a new experience for the character, how would you
describe the differences between the animated world and the real world to him or her?

_____

_____

_____

_____

38. You have been given a magical pencil. Everything you draw with this pencil comes to
life! What do you draw? Tell the story of the things you draw and what you would do with
your newly found power.

_____

_____

_____

_____

                                             ©2012 Build Creative Writing Ideas

Name _____ Date _____

39. If you had a choice to go anywhere in the world with your family
for vacation, where would you go? Don't limit yourself; write about any place in the
world, even if it's somewhere you've never been! Describe your first day in this new place.

_____

_____

_____

_____

_____

40. How did you and your family get to your last vacation? Was it in a plane, a bus or a
car? What about a boat? Write a story about your experience in that mode of transportation
and if it was a good time or not.

_____

_____

_____

_____

_____

©2012 Build Creative Writing Ideas

Name _____ Date _____

41. How do you feel when school lets out for summer vacation and why?

_____

_____

_____

_____

42. What is the best vacation that you have ever gone on? What was so fun about it? Talk about at least three things about that trip that make it stick out in your mind.

_____

_____

_____

_____

 ©2012 Build Creative Writing Ideas

Name _____ Date _____

43. One of the fun things about going on vacation is that you get to try new and exotic foods. Write about a meal you had on vacation in which you tested out a food you'd never had before.

_____

_____

_____

_____

_____

44. While travelling on a big cruise ship, a giant rock causes the ship to crash on a deserted tropical island. Everybody is safe and sound but you have to survive on an island filled with coconuts and sandy beaches. How do you and your family live for a week on this unplanned vacation?

_____

_____

_____

_____

                                              ©2012 Build Creative Writing Ideas

Name _____ Date _____

45. Where do you think movie stars and other famous people go on vacations? What do they do while they are there and what would you do if you got to tag along for a day or two?

_____

_____

_____

_____

46. Due to a change in the way summer vacation works, you and your family only have one day to do your entire vacation. What do you all do on that day to fit in all the fun things of vacation in only 24 hours of time?

_____

_____

_____

_____

 ©2012 Build Creative Writing Ideas

Name _____ Date _____

47. All of your friends' parents have gotten together and have
decided to put you and all of your best friends into a beach house together for the entire
summer. Describe at least three crazy adventures that you all have while living together.

_____

_____

_____

_____

_____

48. Sometimes when a family can't figure out the best place to go for vacation, they do
what's called a "staycation" by staying at home and having a great time. What would you
do on your staycation at home and why?

_____

_____

_____

_____

_____

 ©2012 Build Creative Writing Ideas

Name _____ Date _____

49. What is the most memorable assembly you've ever had at school and why? What did you and your friends say about it after it was over?

_____

_____

_____

_____

50. What are the three craziest places you and your class have gone on a field trip? What did you learn while you were on those trips? Why is a field trip better than learning the same material from a video or book in the classroom?

_____

_____

_____

_____

 ©2012 Build Creative Writing Ideas

Name _____ Date _____

51. Have you ever gotten a chance to leave early from school
because of weather or some other reason? If so, talk about the day when that happened. If not, make up a story in which you have to leave for home in the middle of the day because of school closing a few hours early.

_____

_____

_____

_____

52. What would your school do if the following events happened: alien invasion, giant snow storm, a monkey loose in the school, accidental delivery of 250 pizzas, everybody in the school loses his or her shoes? Write each story separately.

_____

_____

_____

_____

_____

©2012 Build Creative Writing Ideas

Name _____ Date _____

53. What was your favorite day in school of all time? What happened on this day to make it so special?

_____

_____

_____

_____

54. You and your friends have been picked by the principal to come up with an exciting event for your school. What do you decide to do? How can you put together an event that will make everybody happy, both students and teachers?

_____

_____

_____

_____

          ©2012 Build Creative Writing Ideas

Name _____ Date _____

55. What was the toughest thing you ever had to deal with at school?
Was it a difficult test? Was someone a bully? Share your story and try to add as many details as possible.

_____

_____

_____

_____

56. Have you ever had an interesting guest speaker at your school? If so, talk about hearing that person talk and what you learned from it. If not, imagine that one of your favorite famous people in the world came to your school to give a speech. Who is it and why should they talk at your school?

_____

_____

_____

_____

©2012 Build Creative Writing Ideas

Name _____ Date _____

57. If you had the choice, what are five things that you would do to make your school day more exciting? Pretend that you have unlimited money and choices to make these five things happen as soon as possible.

_____

_____

_____

_____

_____

58. What was the best party you've ever had at school? Was it for a holiday like Halloween or something completely different? What did you eat, wear and do?

_____

_____

_____

_____

_____

    ©2012 Build Creative Writing Ideas

Name _____ Date _____

59. What are some of the things that you do for fun around your
house or neighborhood? Do you play video games with friends? Do you shoot hoops in
your own driveway? List at least three things you do and why you like doing them.

_____

_____

_____

_____

_____

60. If you could choose three places to go today in your town to have a good time other
than your house, what would they be? What would you do at these places? Who are the
people you would choose to have there with you?

_____

_____

_____

_____

_____

                                                    ©2012 Build Creative Writing Ideas

Name _____ Date _____

61. Imagine that it's a rainy Saturday at your house and you're not able to go outside. What would you and your family do to pass the time? Start at the beginning of the day and work your way to the end.

_____

_____

_____

_____

62. If you are ever stressed out or grumpy, one of the best ways to deal with that is to find a way to relax. What do you do to relax after a tiring day? What are three things you don't currently do to relax that you might try in the future?

_____

_____

_____

_____

 ©2012 Build Creative Writing Ideas

Name _____ Date _____

63. What are five things that you have done in nature for recreation?
Anything that you do outside counts such as playing football on a grass field or jumping around in a pile of leaves. Pick your favorite of the five and write a story about how enjoyable the activity is to you.

_____

_____

_____

_____

_____

64. When you have recess at school, what are the things you usually do? Are there certain people you typically play with? Write a little story about a memorable day at recess for you.

_____

_____

_____

_____

©2012 Build Creative Writing Ideas

Name _____ Date _____

65. Imagine that your parents and your friends have all come
together to bring you to a crazy theme park with roller coasters, water slides and games!
Describe your day from top to bottom and make sure to talk about all the rides you go on.

_____

_____

_____

_____

66. What is a sport that you and your family might all play together? Might you go for a
bowling night? Rent a boat and go fishing? Even if there is no sport you would all play,
make one up and tell a story of your family playing together.

_____

_____

_____

_____

     ©2012 Build Creative Writing Ideas

Name _____ Date _____

67. One of the best places for recreation is the beach. Have you and
your family ever been to the beach together? If so, describe one of those times in detail. If
not, make up a story about going to the beach and participating in at least three recreational
activities.

_____

_____

_____

_____

_____

68. Imagine that you had an entire year off from school and unlimited money to do
whatever you wanted. What would you do with that year and why? Make sure to write a lot
of ideas because a year without school can seem like a very long time.

_____

_____

_____

_____

_____

©2012 Build Creative Writing Ideas

Name _____ Date _____

69. Imagine that you had a friend or cousin coming in from somewhere far away and you had to show him around your town. What are some of the major sites you would show him? What would you do for fun to demonstrate to him that you live in a cool place?

_____

_____

_____

_____

_____

70. In every country, state and city, there are certain officials that make sure people are following the laws. In each town or city it might be a mayor or a group of officials. Who is the person/persons who run your town and what is it you think they do to keep the streets clean and safe?

_____

_____

_____

_____

©2012 Build Creative Writing Ideas

Name _____ Date _____

71. When a city has something important inside like a lot of people or a big, exciting business, they say that the people or business put the city "on the map." What would you say makes your town or city important enough to be "on the map?" Why would your city be important to other people who live outside of it?

_____

_____

_____

_____

72. Have your parents lived in this city their whole lives or did they come from somewhere else? If they've lived here for a long time, why do you think they like it so much? If they're from somewhere else, where did they come from and why did they end up here?

_____

_____

_____

_____

©2012 Build Creative Writing Ideas

Name _____ Date _____

73. If you left this town to move or for college, what do you think you would miss about it? When you came back to visit, what would be the first place you would go to see? Who would you visit upon your return?

_____

_____

_____

_____

_____

74. Imagine that you were being interviewed by a magazine that figures out the best places to eat, dance and have fun at in your town. Where would you tell them the best place to eat is? What about the best place to dance or have fun? What are some other activities you might mention to the magazine?

_____

_____

_____

_____

_____

 ©2012 Build Creative Writing Ideas

Name _____ Date _____

75. Name and describe the following places you go in your town: grocery store, post office, school, doctor's office, and park.

_____

_____

_____

_____

_____

76. What are some of the places you would go to in town for the following things: seeing a movie, getting a new pair of shoes, going out for dinner on a Friday night, having a birthday party, watching two teams play sports?

_____

_____

_____

_____

_____

©2012 Build Creative Writing Ideas

Name _____ Date _____

77. Imagine that you were the town superhero. You are sworn to protect everyone in town from bad guys and crime. What are some of the crimes you'd stop? Where would you set up your secret headquarters? What would your town-related superhero name be?

_____

_____

_____

_____

_____

78. A time capsule is container that you bury in the ground with select items from the present day. The capsule is to be opened in several decades so that people know what a town was like in the past. If you were in control of this capsule, what would you put in it?

_____

_____

_____

_____

_____

                                          ©2012 Build Creative Writing Ideas

Name _____ Date _____

79. Have you ever had the opportunity to fly in an airplane? If so, what was it like and what were some of the things that impressed you about the experience. If not, tell a story about a possible future plane ride and all of the amazing, interesting things you would see during your trip.

_____

_____

_____

_____

_____

80. When planes were first invented, they could only fit one or two people at a time and they could only go for short distances. What are some of the things you think have changed with technology to make these planes work so much better in the current era?

_____

_____

_____

_____

_____

©2012 Build Creative Writing Ideas

Name _____ Date _____

81. What are some of the other devices that fly other than regular airplanes? Have you ever had the chance to fly in any of them? If so, tell your story. If not, create a story of flying in a non-traditional aircraft and how it makes you feel.

_____

_____

_____

_____

_____

82. Before there were commercial planes, a lot of people took trains to get from point A to point B. Have you ever been on a train? If so, what was it like and how was it different from a car or plane. If not, write a story from your great-grandfather's perspective about what it was like to ride on a train many years ago.

_____

_____

_____

_____

_____

 ©2012 Build Creative Writing Ideas

Name _____ Date _____

83. It's tough to imagine that hundreds if not thousands of people laid down railroad tracks all throughout the country so that a train could get from the East to the West and vice versa. Imagine that you were one of these people working long hours to get the tracks laid down. What would a typical day be like for you?

_____

_____

_____

_____

84. There have been trains in lots of big movies like The Polar Express, Indiana Jones, Harry Potter, Back to the Future and more. Which is your favorite movie train and why? What would it be like to ride on those trains yourself?

_____

_____

_____

_____

   ©2012 Build Creative Writing Ideas

Name _____ Date _____

85. What are the types of cars that your family has? Which of the cars is your favorite to ride in? Do you think that when you're old enough to drive them that you'll get one of them as your first vehicle?

_____

_____

_____

_____

86. If you could create your own car from scratch, what would be some of the new and improved features? What are some of the features you like on normal cars?

_____

_____

_____

_____

 ©2012 Build Creative Writing Ideas

Name _____ Date _____

87. What is the coolest car that you've ever seen in your life? What do you think it would be like to drive it? What would your friends and classmates say if they saw you driving that car?

_____

_____

_____

_____

88. Have you ever had to ride the school bus? What was it like and why did you enjoy it or not enjoy it? What are some of the things that happen on the bus? Would you rather be driven to school or ride on the bus?

_____

_____

_____

_____

©2012 Build Creative Writing Ideas

Name _____ Date _____

89. Imagine that it's a blazingly hot day outside while you're home
for summer vacation. You and your family don't have anything planned for the day. What
do you all do to keep cool and to have a fun time?

_____

_____

_____

_____

90. It is summertime at the community pool. You, your family and your friends are all
hanging out and swimming around to keep the heat at bay. What activities would each
member of your family do during a typical day at the pool?

_____

_____

_____

_____

          ©2012 Build Creative Writing Ideas

Name _____ Date _____

91. Your parents have sent you off to an overnight camp for eight
weeks during the summer. You will be away from most of your friends and you will be in
an unfamiliar place for two months. Then again, you will be sleeping in a cool cabin and
doing fun activities all summer long! Tell a story about this sleep away camp and what you
would do there to pass the time.

_____

_____

_____

_____

92. When you are hot and sweaty during the summer, one of the best things to do is to
drink a refreshing, chilly beverage. What is your drink of choice during the summer and
why? Do you buy it at a store or make it yourself? Would you consider selling the drink at
a refreshing drink stand?

_____

_____

_____

_____

©2012 Build Creative Writing Ideas

Name _____ Date _____

93. During a regular summer day, what would your usual attire be?
Are you a shorts and a t-shirt kind of person? Do you always have a swimsuit underneath so you're ready to jump in a pool or run through some sprinklers? Do you stay in your pajamas to play video games? Go into detail of your outfit from top to bottom.

_____

_____

_____

_____

_____

94. What are some of the most fun summer activities you've ever done? Some examples might include swimming in the ocean, hiking up a mountain or sliding down a hill on a block of ice. Tell at least three stories of summer activities. If you have not done anything too exciting, make up a story in which you get to do three crazy activities in one day.

_____

_____

_____

_____

      ©2012 Build Creative Writing Ideas

Name _____ Date _____

95. Name at least three sports that you and your friends might play
during the summer? Who is the best of your friends at these sports and why do you enjoy
playing them so much?

_____

_____

_____

_____

_____

96. During the summer, a lot of families embark on a summer road trip. This might be a
trip to see your relatives or it might be on the way to an exciting vacation. Tell a story (real
or made-up) about a family road trip to a cool destination.

_____

_____

_____

_____

_____

 ©2012 Build Creative Writing Ideas

Name _____ Date _____

97. While some people just sit around all summer, others take the time off to do something cool like read a number of books or paint a painting. What are five productive, interesting things you could do during your next summer vacation and why would you want to do them in particular?

_____

_____

_____

_____

_____

98. Imagine that you lived in a part of the country that had a really short summer, where there were only a few days of warmth surrounded by over 300 cold days. How would your summer be different and how would you take advantage of the warmth for that short period of time?

_____

_____

_____

_____

 ©2012 Build Creative Writing Ideas

Name _____ Date _____

99. Try to remember back to the first time you ever saw snow. What was it like seeing it for the first time and then touching it for the first time? Were you surprised at all? Did you like it at the time or were you not a fan?

_____

_____

_____

_____

100. Have you ever had to walk around in a huge winter snow storm? If so, what was it like and how difficult was it? If not, create a story about having to trudge through over a foot of snow in your backyard and around your house.

_____

_____

_____

_____

©2012 Build Creative Writing Ideas

Name _____ Date _____

101. One of the best ways to warm up after a few hours in the snow
is to put on some warm socks, drink a hot chocolate and sit by the fireplace. Whether or
not you've had the pleasure of doing that, tell a story about warming up in this way and
how good it feels.

_____

_____

_____

_____

102. How does the winter in your town compare with the winters in other towns? Is there
more snow here than anywhere else? Is it relatively mild? How is it different?

_____

_____

_____

_____

                                         ©2012 Build Creative Writing Ideas

Name _____ Date _____

103. Have you ever been involved in a snow ball fight? If so, talk
about how it went and if there were any winners and losers. If not, create a story in which
there is a huge snow ball fight between you and your friends.

_____

_____

_____

_____

_____

104. The winter season brings a lot of fun holiday cheer both inside and outside of school.
Do you enjoy all of the bright lights and presents of the winter? Why or why not?

_____

_____

_____

_____

 ©2012 Build Creative Writing Ideas

Name _____ Date _____

105. What kind of outfit do you wear for a snowy and cold winter's day? Do you have a big, puffy coat and boots? Go into detail about every part of the outfit from your wool hat down to your thick socks.

_____

_____

_____

_____

_____

106. What are some of the animals that you might see during the winter that you wouldn't see any other part of the year? If you're not sure that you've seen any animals in the winter, make up a story in which you see your favorite cold region animals (like penguins and polar bears) walking through your backyard!

_____

_____

_____

_____

_____

 ©2012 Build Creative Writing Ideas

Name _____ Date _____

107. Imagine that you, Frosty the Snowman, Rudolph the Red Nosed
Reindeer and Jack Frost have to go on a mission to save somebody that is stuck in his
house from a blizzard. How do you meet these wintry creatures and how do you go about
your mission?

_____

_____

_____

_____

108. One of the toughest parts of winter is the ice. This is the ice that you can slip on and
that your parents' cars can slip on Why are icy conditions so dangerous during the winter
and what do people normally do about it to be more safe?

_____

_____

_____

_____

 ©2012 Build Creative Writing Ideas

Name _____ Date _____

109. Why is Fall called Fall? Tell a story of hundreds of years ago when people decided to call the season Fall and why they did it.

_____

_____

_____

_____

110. Imagine going on a drive down a street with lots of trees. You see the beautiful foliage of the leaves with colors like red, brown, green and yellow. Describe your feelings about the bright and pretty colors plastered throughout the forest during your drive.

_____

_____

_____

_____

Name _____ Date _____

111. Your parents have spent the last few hours raking all of the
leaves into a giant pile. When they aren't looking, you dive into the pile, scattering the leaves every which way. They look right at you when you exit the pile. What happens next?

_____

_____

_____

_____

112. Lots of cool events happen during the fall, like Halloween, the start of football season and Thanksgiving. What is your favorite fall event and why?

_____

_____

_____

_____

©2012 Build Creative Writing Ideas

Name _____ Date _____

113. What is the weather during fall like in your town? What do you
think it would be like in a place much farther south? What about in a place much farther
north? What about on the other side of the world?

_____

_____

_____

_____

114. Imagine life as a little leaf on a tree. You grew up all spring and summer and now
you're getting ready to jump down to the ground in the fall. Tell your leafy story from
beginning to end, including what happens after you fall.

_____

_____

_____

_____

                                                    ©2012 Build Creative Writing Ideas

Name _____ Date _____

115. In some ancient cultures, when there was no scientific explanation for something, they would make up a myth or an origin story of how something came to be. Create a myth about how and why the leaves started changing colors and falling.

_____

_____

_____

_____

116. If you could get all of your friends together to do one huge fall activity what would it be and why? Tell the story of you and your friends doing this activity together from beginning to end.

_____

_____

_____

_____

©2012 Build Creative Writing Ideas

Name _____ Date _____

117. What are some of the things you don't like about the fall season? If you could change any three things about it what would they be? How would fall be different with these new things in place?

_____

_____

_____

_____

118. What are your favorite foods of the fall season? List at least five your favorite fall-related dishes (for example, pumpkin pie) and talk about the last time that you ate each one. Remember to give credit to the chef!

_____

_____

_____

_____

 ©2012 Build Creative Writing Ideas

Name _____ Date _____

119. How do you know when spring really starts? Is it the first blossom from a bush or tree? Is it the reappearance of squirrels and other forest animals? Other than using the calendar, how do you really know that spring is on its way?

_____

_____

_____

_____

_____

120. What would the end of winter into the beginning of spring be like for you if you were an animal living in the woods? Would you and your animal buddies have a party when it got warmer?

_____

_____

_____

_____

_____

 ©2012 Build Creative Writing Ideas

Name _____ Date _____

121. There are a lot of fun things that happen in the spring like baseball spring training, warmer temperatures and longer daylight hours than winter. What is your favorite part of the spring and why?

_____

_____

_____

_____

_____

122. One part of Spring requires a lot of hard work and effort and that part is Spring Cleaning. This is a day when your parents make you stay inside and work hard even when it's nice outside. Imagine that you are forced to clean for this event while your friends are all playing outside. Write a story about that day.

_____

_____

_____

_____

_____

Name _____ Date _____

123. What is your typical spring outfit like? How is it different from your many-layered winter outfit? If you had unlimited money at your disposal, what additions would you make to this outfit?

_____

_____

_____

_____

124. When it comes to Daylight Savings Time, the phrase usually goes "spring forward, fall back." What does that mean you have to do in the spring? How do you spring forward and what are some of the consequences of springing forward?

_____

_____

_____

_____

Name _____ Date _____

125. Now that it's spring again, you and your friends have the ability
to do all sorts of activities you couldn't do during the winter. What are your top three
activities? Write a story about a specific time you and your friends did one of the three
things.

_____

_____

_____

_____

_____

126. One of the most predominant colors of spring is green. The newly grown plants are
green, some of the holidays (like St. Patrick's Day) are green and a lot of the clothing has
green in it. Imagine if spring suddenly adopted a new color and now everything was
purple, orange or some other color. How would things change?

_____

_____

_____

_____

 ©2012 Build Creative Writing Ideas

Name _____ Date _____

127. Spring is a sort of re-birth from all the cold of winter. Some
people take it as a time to start a new habit like an exercise plan or by writing every day.
What is a new habit that you can start up in the spring and why would you choose that in
particular?

_____

_____

_____

_____

_____

128. What is your favorite spring animal that you see around your town now that it's
warm? If you could have a conversation with that animal, what would it be about and why?

_____

_____

_____

_____

_____

                              ©2012 Build Creative Writing Ideas

Name _____ Date _____

129. Which is your favorite of the four seasons and why? What do you do during that season that makes it so special to you?

_____

_____

_____

_____

130. Which is your least favorite of the four seasons and why? What are some things you could do during the season to make it more exciting and interesting?

_____

_____

_____

_____

     ©2012 Build Creative Writing Ideas

Name _____ Date _____

131. Imagine that you are an animal living outside through all four seasons. Which animal are you? How do you survive through all of the different seasons out in the wild?

_____

_____

_____

_____

_____

132. You have been given the job of making a brand new 12 month calendar with new seasons. What would you change? Would you change any names of the months or the seasons? How do you think people would react to your new way of doing things?

_____

_____

_____

_____

_____

          ©2012 Build Creative Writing Ideas

Name _____ Date _____

133. How would the different seasons affect people in the following professions: firefighter, ice cream man, gardener, airplane pilot, ship captain?

_____

_____

_____

_____

134. A rain storm can happen during any of the seasons, but it can be a lot different depending on the temperature. How is a rain storm in the summer different from a rain storm in the winter? Go into detail and pull from your own experiences.

_____

_____

_____

_____

 ©2012 Build Creative Writing Ideas

Name _____ Date _____

135. In other parts of the world, the seasons can be a lot different.
Write a story in which you explain to someone from another country how the four seasons are in your town.

_____

_____

_____

_____

_____

136. Why do you think that the earth has four seasons? Why doesn't it just stay summer all year round? What do you think would happen if it was just sunny and warm all the time?

_____

_____

_____

_____

_____

 ©2012 Build Creative Writing Ideas

Name _____ Date _____

137. One of the best parts of the warmer seasons is that there are some amazing fruits to pick straight off the tree. Have you ever been fruit picking? If so, write a story about your family's trip to an orchard. If not, create a tale about picking some wild and exotic fruit to make into a fresh pie.

_____

_____

_____

_____

_____

138. Of all the 12 months, which would you say is the one that you enjoy the most? Is it because of a particular season or a particular holiday? Give lots of reasons why and tell a little story about when it became your favorite month.

_____

_____

_____

_____

_____

 ©2012 Build Creative Writing Ideas

Name _____ Date _____

139. The way you describe a person who is between a "friend" and a "stranger" is often called an "acquaintance." This is somebody you have met, but that you don't know well enough to call a friend. List five acquaintances in your life and describe how you know them and the way that they act toward you.

_____

_____

_____

_____

140. Do you and your family have any "family friends?" These are people who aren't related to you but who come over all the time and are practically like family. If so, write a story about you and your family hanging out with the family friend. If not, create a tale about an entertaining family friend who comes over to your house for dinner.

_____

_____

_____

_____

 ©2012 Build Creative Writing Ideas

Name _____ Date _____

141. Have you ever felt shy when your parents have introduced you
to a new person? Describe what that experience was like and why you think you felt that
way.

_____

_____

_____

_____

_____

142. Imagine that you are trapped in an elevator with five people that you don't know. It
will take the maintenance crew at least an hour to get you out of there safely. What do you
and the five strangers talk about while you're stuck?

_____

_____

_____

_____

_____

 ©2012 Build Creative Writing Ideas

Name _____ Date _____

143. Who of the following people do you enjoy the most and why:
family doctor, housekeeper or nanny, delivery person, grocery store checkout person or
swim/music/dance instructor?

_____

_____

_____

_____

_____

144. Who is the most interesting person you've ever met? Whether this is a friend, a family
member or a complete stranger, go into detail about why this person was so interesting.

_____

_____

_____

_____

_____

©2012 Build Creative Writing Ideas

Name _____ Date _____

145. Imagine that you and one of your parents or siblings sit down
on an airplane next to a person who loves talking. What do you and the "super talker" talk
about? Write a dialogue between you, your relative and the talking person.

_____

_____

_____

_____

_____

146. You and your class have decided to write to pen pals in a foreign country of your
choice! Pen pals are kids close to your age who are in a completely different culture and
country who you can write to. What country do you choose and what do you write in your
first letter to your pen pal?

_____

_____

_____

_____

 ©2012 Build Creative Writing Ideas

Name _____ Date _____

147. Who is the strangest person you've ever met? What did this person do to seem so weird to you?

_____

_____

_____

_____

148. You have been chosen to speak about your favorite subject in front of a room of 150 strangers. What is the topic you will discuss? How do you feel about being in front of so many people you don't know? How does the speech go?

_____

_____

_____

_____

                    ©2012 Build Creative Writing Ideas

Name _____ Date _____

149. What are some of the ways that you use the Internet on a daily basis? Do you use it at home or at school? Do your parents use it in their jobs? Why do you think it is or is not important in your life?

_____

_____

_____

_____

_____

150. Imagine a world in which the Internet was never invented. How would your life change? How would you look things up for homework or projects?

_____

_____

_____

_____

_____

 ©2012 Build Creative Writing Ideas

Name _____ Date _____

151. One of the things you can do using the Internet is to send funny videos and articles to other people. What is the funniest thing you've ever seen on the Internet and why? Tell the story of the first time you saw it.

_____

_____

_____

_____

152. Do your parents put any restrictions on your use of the Internet? If so, what do they restrict? Do you think it's a good idea to limit your time or the sites that you are allowed to look at? If there are no restrictions, do you think that you would put restrictions on your kids' Internet use when you're a parent?

_____

_____

_____

_____

 ©2012 Build Creative Writing Ideas

Name _____ Date _____

153. Some people spend all their time sending viruses and spam mail throughout the Internet. Why do you think people do that? What would you do if you met one of these virus and spam-sending people in person?

_____

_____

_____

_____

_____

154. What are five things that you like about the Internet? What are five things that you dislike about the Internet? If you had the choice, what would you change to make the five things you dislike about the Internet much better?

_____

_____

_____

_____

 ©2012 Build Creative Writing Ideas

Name _____ Date _____

155. What are your five favorite websites on the Internet? What do you like about them? If you had to write a thank you note to the creator of one of the websites, what would you say?

_____

_____

_____

_____

156. What are some of the most important things that you still cannot do on the Internet? Do you think they'll ever figure out how to make these things digital and online or do you believe they will always have to be in the real world?

_____

_____

_____

_____

 ©2012 Build Creative Writing Ideas

Name _____ Date _____

157. Sometimes people use the Internet for bad things like bullying.
What are five good and positive things you could use the Internet for? Go into extreme detail and create a plan for at least one of them.

_____

_____

_____

_____

_____

158. Right now, some of the most popular websites on the Internet are Google, Facebook and Twitter. Create a new idea for a website that will be the most popular website 50 years from now. Describe the website and write about why you think so many people will want to use it.

_____

_____

_____

_____

_____

                                              ©2012 Build Creative Writing Ideas

Name _____ Date _____

159. Imagine that you have been contacted by an encyclopedia that wants to create an entry about you! Write your own biography that lists your accomplishments, your activities, your personal qualities and anything else you can think of.

_____

_____

_____

_____

160. What is a time in your life that you felt extremely proud about yourself and something that you did? Explain why it made you feel so proud and if you'll ever do anything like it again.

_____

_____

_____

_____

                                             ©2012 Build Creative Writing Ideas

Name _____ Date _____

161. List five goals for yourself. Goals are things that you want to achieve at some point during your lifetime. An example of a goal might be, "I want to swim the English Channel" or "I want to write a book." Explain why these are goals for you and how you plan to make them happen.

_____

_____

_____

_____

_____

162. We all change a lot from the time we're a baby until now. How have you changed personally? Obviously you are taller and bigger, but what are some of the other ways you've changed and grown since infancy?

_____

_____

_____

_____

Name _____ Date _____

163. In school, you usually get grades for class subjects like spelling, reading and math. What if you got grades for the kind of person you were in areas like kindness, friendship and happiness? Come up with five categories related to life and give yourself a letter grade (A for the best, F for failing) and a reason why you received that grade.

_____

_____

_____

_____

_____

164. Imagine that the future version of you, from five years from now, met with you at a restaurant for lunch. What would you two talk about? What would the future version of you have to tell you about what's going to happen in your life in the next five years?

_____

_____

_____

_____

            ©2012 Build Creative Writing Ideas

Name _____ Date _____

165. If you had an opportunity to change some things about your personality and the way you treat people, what would they be and why? How would you change these things and how long would they take?

_____

_____

_____

_____

_____

166. They say that you never really understand somebody until they "walk a mile in your shoes." What do you think somebody would learn about you if they became you for an entire day? Describe that person's day in which they are dressed like, look like and need to act like you.

_____

_____

_____

_____

_____

 ©2012 Build Creative Writing Ideas

Name _____ Date _____

167. List out five things you think you'll do in each of the following settings: middle school, high school, college, your first job.

_____

_____

_____

_____

_____

168. How would you have turned out different if you were born 20 years in the past? How would you be different if you were born 20 years in the future? Go into excessive detail.

_____

_____

_____

_____

_____

 ©2012 Build Creative Writing Ideas

Name _____ Date _____

169. You have just walked into a spooky house! What is in the
spooky house? Are there any people in the house? What do they say to you?

_____

_____

_____

_____

_____

170. What is something you love to do more than anything else in the world? Why do you
like it so much?

_____

_____

_____

_____

_____

          ©2012 Build Creative Writing Ideas

Name _____ Date _____

171. What is your favorite book or television show? Talk about a funny scene in and what the characters say to each other.

_____

_____

_____

_____

172. You have found a magic wand! You can do anything with it. What do you do? Do you share the wand with anybody else?

_____

_____

_____

_____

 ©2012 Build Creative Writing Ideas

Name _____ Date _____

173. Your mom and dad buy you a new big dog as a Christmas
present! Talk about the dog. What does the dog do? What does he look like?

_____

_____

_____

_____

174. What do you want to be when you grow up and why? Who is the most famous person
who has that job already? If you don't know, make him up!

_____

_____

_____

_____

 ©2012 Build Creative Writing Ideas

Name _____ Date _____

175. Write about your teacher! What is your teacher's name, what does he or she look like, and what do you like about him or her?

_____

_____

_____

_____

176. What is your favorite food? Who makes it better your mom, dad, or a restaurant? Talk about the food and what makes it so good.

_____

_____

_____

_____

 ©2012 Build Creative Writing Ideas

Name _____ Date _____

177. What do your mom and dad do for work? What do they do for fun?

_____

_____

_____

_____

178. What is your house like? What do you like the most about it? What is your favorite room in the house?

_____

_____

_____

_____

                                        ©2012 Build Creative Writing Ideas

Name _____ Date _____

179. You have had a magic spell cast on you and you are now 30 years old! What do you do now that you don't go to school anymore? Do you get a job? Do you get married?

_____

_____

_____

_____

180. Who is your favorite famous person? What do you like about him or her and would you like to do what he or she does when you grow up? Why?

_____

_____

_____

_____

 ©2012 Build Creative Writing Ideas

Name _____ Date _____

181. If you could be a character in any book or movie who would it
be? What would you do differently and what would you do the same as the character?
Why?

_____

_____

_____

_____

182. What is your favorite thing to do during the summer? Is it camp? Going on a
vacation? Hanging out in the house? Why do you like it so much?

_____

_____

_____

_____

 ©2012 Build Creative Writing Ideas

Name _____ Date _____

183. What do you think your parents were like when they were your age? Do you think they were the same as you or different from you? Would you and your parents have been friends?

_____

_____

_____

_____

184. What is the scariest thing that's ever happened to you? Why was it so scary and how did you deal with it?

_____

_____

_____

_____

            ©2012 Build Creative Writing Ideas

Name _____ Date _____

185. How big is your family? Talk a little bit about everybody in
your family: brothers, sisters, grandparents, cousins, uncles. Talk about everybody!

_____

_____

_____

_____

186. What is your favorite subject in school? Do you like reading the most? Do you like
Math or Science? Talk about that subject and why you like it so much.

_____

_____

_____

_____

 ©2012 Build Creative Writing Ideas

Name _____ Date _____

187. Talk about a fun thing you did with your friends or family.
Write about the day from the time you woke up to the time you went to sleep. What did you like so much about it?

_____

_____

_____

_____

_____

188. What do you think you could do to help out in your town? How could you make things better for everybody else? Write about how even one person can make a difference.

_____

_____

_____

_____

_____

 ©2012 Build Creative Writing Ideas

Name _____ Date _____

189. If you had to write a book what would it be about? Talk about
some of the characters from the book and what they would be doing.

_____

_____

_____

_____

190. Your teacher has made you the teacher for the rest of the week. What are you going to
teach the rest of the class about? Do you think you would be a good teacher? How do you
think the class will feel about you being the teacher?

_____

_____

_____

_____

 ©2012 Build Creative Writing Ideas

Name _____ Date _____

191. Writers have referred to nature as "the great outdoors." Why do
you think they've talked about it like that? What are some of the things that make nature
"great?"

_____

_____

_____

_____

192. One author, named Henry David Thoreau lived out in nature for a long time and wrote
a book about his experiences. Imagine that you were spending a year or two out in nature.
How would you live there? What are the things you would miss about living in your
house? What are the things you wouldn't miss?

_____

_____

_____

_____

                                        ©2012 Build Creative Writing Ideas

Name _____ Date _____

193. In animated features like Cinderella, a whistle and a song bring on dozens of little animal friends to help out the main character. What would your life be like if you had friends throughout the forest to help you on your way? Which animals would they be and how did you become friends?

_____

_____

_____

_____

194. There are many potential threats to the environment like pollution and deforestation. Some people even believe that the environment will be damaged beyond repair for your generation. What could you do to keep the environment safe for you and future generations?

_____

_____

_____

_____

 ©2012 Build Creative Writing Ideas

Name _____ Date _____

195. Talk about a time in which you and your friends or you and your family went out into nature. What did you see? What did you learn?

_____

_____

_____

_____

196. Imagine that you, your family and your friends all went into nature to hike up a big mountain. Who would be there and what would their reaction be to the hard work and beautiful scenery? How often would you do this sort of thing if you had a choice?

_____

_____

_____

_____

 ©2012 Build Creative Writing Ideas

Name _____ Date _____

197. Have you ever been to the ocean? If so, what were your feelings
the first time you saw that vast body of water? If not, create a story in which you see the
ocean and play around on the beach for the first time.

_____

_____

_____

_____

198. In your lifetime, what are some of the more exotic natural locations you want to go?
Would you go to the rainforest or to the Arctic Circle? List at least five different natural
habitats. Pick one and then write a story about your trip there.

_____

_____

_____

_____

Name _____ Date _____

199. Pick your favorite wild animal. Create a story in which you become that animal for a day and have to figure out how to survive in your natural environment. Write about what you eat, what you do and what other animals you hang out with.

_____

_____

_____

_____

200. Some people believe that nature has become less important for us as technology has become more advanced. Do you think nature is still important to you and the future generations? Why do you believe that?

_____

_____

_____

_____

                    ©2012 Build Creative Writing Ideas

Extra Page

Name _____ Date _____

_____

_____

_____

_____

_____

_____

_____

_____

_____

                                          ©2012 Build Creative Writing Ideas

ABOUT THE AUTHOR

Bryan Cohen is a writer, actor and director who grew up in Dresher, Pennsylvania just outside of Philadelphia. He graduated from the University of North Carolina at Chapel Hill with degrees in English and Dramatic Art along with a minor in Creative Writing. His books on writing prompts and writing motivation have sold over 10,000 copies and they include *1,000 Creative Writing Prompts: Ideas for Blogs, Scripts, Stories and More*, *1,000 Character Writing Prompts: Villains, Heroes and Hams for Scripts, Stories and More*, *500 Writing Prompts for Kids: First Grade through Fifth Grade*, *1,000 Character Writing Prompts: Villains, Heroes and Hams for Scripts, Stories and More* and *The Post-College Guide to Happiness*. Cohen continues to produce and perform plays and films in between his books and freelance writing work. He lives in Chicago.

31556780R00065

Made in the USA
Lexington, KY
16 April 2014